IMAGE OF AN ISLAND

No — not old — the island is young.
As young as innocence and faith,
As young as throwing a net for fish
With the awkward grace of a boy.
As clean as sunlight on cloud,
As cloud-blue delicate as fawn in flight.

Truth is not still, is not idle —
The ocean moves.
The child smiles.
The mother loves — The mother protects.
Night comes
The water loses its reflections until the dawn.

Truth is beautiful,
    — is not beautiful,
The sails swell like a woman with child.
Sun blackens the skin
    — whitens bones.
Man shaped his shrines like a woman's breast.
He built lakes in which to catch the moon
    — and drowned the trees.

Olga Delgado

IMAGE OF AN ISLAND

A PORTRAIT OF CEYLON

by Reg van Cuylenburg

ORION PRESS

NEW YORK

ACKNOWLEDGEMENTS

I share this book with many people who helped make it a reality. To all of them I extend my thanks and gratitude, particularly to the following:

To Jimmy Greenshields and Chandra Arulpragasem who journeyed with me several times to the oldest and remotest jungle water-holes.

To Happuwa of Manampitiya who took me to a rookery on the banks of the Maha Velli Ganga, that few men know of.

To Mr. Talwatte, a fine old Kandyan gentleman, who gave me the opportunity of photographing the Raja Maha Perahera at Kandy.

To all my American friends, particularly those at 46th Street, who were understanding and made the coffee at midnight, during long sessions of editing contact-sheets; and to Axel Grosser who made such perfect prints, from my negatives, some of which were slightly the worse for wear.

Lastly to Olga Delgado who wrote the poem which conveys the meaning of, and perhaps, part of the reason why, I took these pictures.

R. v. C.
September, 1961

For Irma

"Betwixt mine Eye and Heart a League is took
And each doth good turns now unto the other"

William Shakespeare,
Sonnets

INTRODUCTION

Here in New York, as I watch the snow swirl down 46th Street, my mind goes back along the crooked path of memory to another land, where snow is unknown and sky-scrapers would be regarded with benign curiosity. I remember one day long ago, when I watched the rain, as I now watch the snow. I was in boarding school then, and had been sent to the sickroom with malaria. It was August and the Rugger season was in full swing, but while other people scrounged in the mud of the playing fields, I sat with my nose pressed against the window-pane, watching the rain. The clouds built up like castles over the peak of Hantané, and thunder grumbled across the valley. The sky grew dark, and suddenly the world became sad; then with a crashing roar lightning flickered across the sky and the rain came down, a solid sheet of water that hit the earth with the force of a fist. I had a camera then, a Zeiss Box Tengor, with Waterhouse stops, and a malicious shutter. I took a picture of the rain but it didn't come out the way I wanted.

Years later, long after the wicked shutter of the Tengor had broken with a hideous twanging noise, I became the proud possessor of a Leica model III. My friend Jimmy owned an Exacta and as often as possible we would escape from Colombo to the jungle and the sea, far from typewriters and taxicabs.

It was here that we found the real Ceylon, removed from the diseased values of "civilization," steeped in legend and whimsy. The idea of a book was born, and I set to work in earnest. Jimmy and I shared many moments of high adventure and hilarious nonsense. We used to set off in his little black Morris Minor, a stout-hearted car, pos-sessed of weird mechanical complications and a devilish sense of humor. We drove her everywhere, along cart-tracks into the jungle, up dry river-beds into mangrove swamps, and along the coast in search of fishing villages. She used to suffer from carburetor trouble much as humans suffer from indigestion. When an attack seized her she would stop dead, and Jimmy would disappear under her bonnet, armed with a tool-kit. Presently there came grinding noises, indicative of some painful surgery, and she would bleed black oil all over the clean jungle road. Jimmy would appear with a smudged face, clutching a piece of severed hose that looked like an amputated organ, climb in and press the starter-button. She would gather herself together like a cat preparing to spring, and with an ear-splitting backfire, leap forward and away we'd go, clattering like a gypsy caravan full of tin pots.

Food was our big problem, for on trips like ours one had to be prepared to eat anything. Jimmy was a Scotsman, and though there flowed in his veins the rugged strength of his splendid ancestors, he had been brought up on such relatively harmless things as haggis and whisky. Apart from Sunday lunches of mild curry he had never attempted our somewhat searing cuisine. I remember once we stopped for breakfast at a little roadside village, where a nut-brown girl baked "hoppers" over a wood-fire. These are wafer-thin cakes made of rice-flour, and she offered us some with a chili-and-salt sambol. Jimmy decided to try some though I warned him that the sambol would be hot. After the second mouthful his face flushed. He looked at me and remarked with a blistered tongue, "Pretty powerful stuff, don't you think?" He was a brave soul, and no man could have wished for a better friend.

Our experiences were many, and the tricks played on us by that perverse black car were legion. Like the time we drove her across a shallow jungle stream and her head-lamps filled with water. Ever after she glared at the world like a drunken cod.

Those days were happy ones, and passed quickly, for happiness is a fleeting thing, lighting the darkness of life as an oil-wick lights a shrine. There was much to do, bulk film to be loaded into cassettes, exposed film to be processed, negatives to be filed and edited. All this against the day when tiny squares of film could be enlarged to the $11'' \times 14''$ pictures, which when put together would form my image of my island. Soon my little darkroom was bulging with the material of a happy labor and, with each batch of negatives filed away in empty shoe-boxes, the image grew and became more meaningful.

I have been told by other, more experienced, authors that the first book is the greatest thrill. Perhaps this is true and, if it is, I can understand it. Like the first love —pure and fresh, delicious with discovery and excitement. But now that it is finished, and I sit here watching the snow and idly turning over proof-pages, I could close my eyes and the memories of unphotographable things come crowding my mind. The smell of burning camphor at Kataragama, the creak and thud of bullock-carts on a village road, the haunting lilt of a lullaby, hanging for a second in the heavy night air, and then lost in silence as a mother lays her baby to rest.

Now I know why Adam came to Lanka, when he was driven from the Garden of Eden . . .

ᎢᏏᎬ ᎳᎬᎯᏞᎢᏏ ᎤᎰ ᎳᎯᎢᎬᎡ

Water is a thing of magic, the giver of life and the fountain from which our very energy springs, to be nourished and refreshed, so long as we live. It is the thing we remember most when in strange lands our thoughts turn to home, and we recall the names of rivers and the seasons of past years. We remember the quality of rain, and the mood of it, for in each land these are different, dependent on wind and cloud and sun. The rain that comes to Lanka is no miserly drizzle, but a furious living thing that stings and lashes like a carter's whip. When the storm is over, and the earth lies steaming in the sun, the monsoon forgets its fury, and water acquires a new gentleness. A miracle happens and muddy pools beget a new reflection, and tired streams a new sparkle to their splash.

Possibly this condition prevails because ours is an island home, and our water sucked from an emerald ocean and rolled into castellated clouds, which are hurled by the monsoon winds against the hills of Uda Rata, to collapse ragged and spent. It leaves the rain forest dark and dripping, full of misty ghosts of past warrior-kings, and the muffled laughter of a forest stream which is persistent and mutters along its way, sliding into the ravines and tumbling down the sheer rock faces till it reaches level ground, quivering from the exertions of a long journey. Gently it is tapped by a Sinhalese farmer who changes its course and runs it into the "wewa" which feeds his fields. Here it justifies its existence, and because of it the farmer is able to plough and grow the rice which sustains his village. However, it is the stream and not the farmer that can lay claim to some kind of permanent existence. For centuries the stream with its muffled laughter has flowed into the fields of the village and mirrored the life of its toiling inhabitants.

The "wewa" is to a Sinhalese village what a Mayfair club is to a Guards officer. Many years ago a Sinhalese king declared that "not a drop of water shall fall on Lanka, but that it serves man." To give truth to his statement he strung a bund across a valley, changed the course of a river, and created a man-made lake, thousands of acres in extent. In the lee of the lake he built a splendid city of broad roads and granite palaces. But wealth and power bring their own destruction and the jungle rose and covered the work of his architects. The lake became the resting place of other forest folk.

This is the story of many of the village "wewas," and the people who live in their lee are probably the descendants of the very architects who designed the scattered ruins in the jungle. Today the "wewa" is meeting-place, town-hall, lovers' tryst, and bathing place.

In the morning the girls come down to bathe. The purpose of the bath is not merely to keep clean—it is to gossip and chatter, to talk of lovers and swains, and to delight the eye of anybody who may pass by. They pour potfuls of water on their heads—so many for good luck, so many for good health, and so many to "keep the body cool." Their grace would be the envy of a ballerina and their youth and charm are ageless.

The water from the wewa, having fed the fields and fallen from the brown backs of the bathing girls, flows into the little stream which eventually meets a broad brown river, fringed with yellow bamboo and knotted rain-trees. The sand of the bank is fine as talc, warm with the early sun, and orange-gold. Mahouts bring their elephants to bathe here and this is the place to enjoy a quiet chuckle. Of all the animals in all the world the elephant is the gentlest and the most lovable. In captivity they must be tended with care and treated with respect. They have their own language which the mahout must learn before he can control them. Once the language has been learned and man and beast understand each other, a lifelong friendship develops. Like all friendships it is a matter of give and take on both sides. Little disagreements flare up on either side. There are moments of rebellion, hurt, and sometimes even an exhibition of the sulks. But the bond is very strong, and I have often had the whimsical thought that world leaders would do well to take a few lessons from the elephants that lie at peace in the cool water of our river, while their mahouts talk of the day's doings.

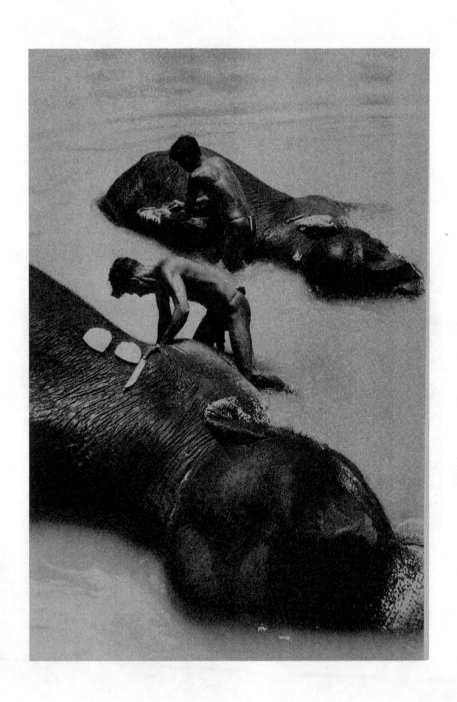

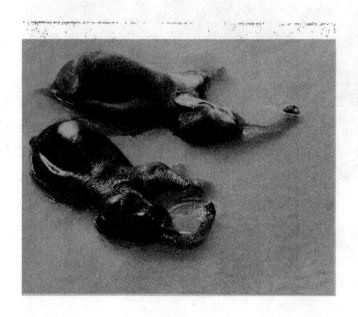

ROAD TO A VILLAGE

Off every main road that cuts a black, tarred scar through the glaring green of the landscape, a red gravel path turns into the trees and winds lazily into a village. Areca-nut palms flank both sides of this dusty rutted path, rising as slender as swizzle-sticks, topped with incongruous tufts of bottle-green leaves. Through the underbrush, if the village borders on the jungle, deer tread with caution as they investigate the possibility of raiding the fields of young Indian corn. Beyond lie the rice-fields, neat and geometrical, like a carpet of emerald-green velvet, a testimony to the orderly habits of man that contrasts sharply with the wild splendor of the surrounding jungle. The road continues, past the rice-fields to the cluster of huts that form the village. Fat brown children play in the shade of spreading bread-fruit trees and long lean pi-dogs lie dozing in the heat of noonday. Women and young girls pound rice or tend the small vegetable garden at the back of each hut, where they grow purple brinjals, and fat yellow pumpkins. The land is rich, and each garden is full of a variety of plants and trees. Coconut palms and plantain trees, chillie-plants, and pepper-vines for food, and for decoration bushes of hibiscus and croton, and trees of jacaranda and jasmine.

Every village has an ancient tamarind or mango tree, and it is near here that the village shopkeeper does business. Of all the village folk he is the most prosperous. He keeps bags of rice and rock salt, piles of dhal and red onions, long sticks of maldive fish. He is used to bargaining with the womenfolk and though his tongue is tart when it comes to credit, his heart is kind to the children, for whom he has a huge supply of sticky sweetmeats.

The village exists because of the fields and the "wewa" which feeds them. This is where the Sinhalese farmer works, ploughing, turning, sowing, season after season, while each year the sun tans his body to a copper-brown, and the monsoon floods his fields and turns the indolent village stream into a boiling river. Everybody awaits the harvest time, and women and children help to thresh and winnow the grain.

After harvest the village gives thanks. There is now time to sit in the sun and gossip, to read a newspaper, to go to the town and watch the Perahera and, on poya-nights, to go to the temple and offer flowers. Of course it is the children and the young girls who most of all look forward to the journey into town. There are saris to be bought, fortune-tellers to be consulted over matters of the heart, relatives to visit.

When the Perahera is over, and the bazaar keepers have taken down their stalls and moved away, the farmer and his family return along the dusty red road to the village. It is good to be home, among one's own kind; besides, there is work to be done in the fields. The neeras of the fields have to be repaired, ploughs mended, coconuts to be plucked, jak-trees to be felled. But the visit to town has changed the lives of a few. Did not the fortune-teller prophesy to Nirmala that she would meet a handsome young fellow near the river bank before the waning of the moon? She knows exactly who it will be, too. Recently she noticed that Appuhamy's son, the tall one with the haughty head and a body as slim and lithe as a sword-blade, would hang around the very spot where she would soak the coconut leaves. Nirmala knows that he is for her, and their marriage will add another hut to the village, and by-and-by another nut-brown toddler to splash and romp in the river.

So life goes on. The monsoon follows drought, and Nirmala will soon be worried over the choice of a suitable girl for her young son, whose head is held high and whose body is lithe as a sword-blade.

Outside, the deer tread with caution through the underbrush and the dust rises from the red road . . .

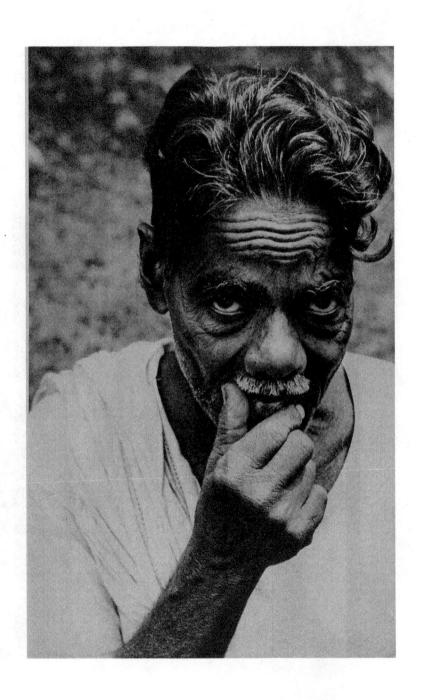

BY ROYAL COMMAND

Kandy is a place that invites envy. It is far too old, far too beautiful and far too contented. It was not always so, for there was a time when the Kandyans lived a more adventurous life than their descendants of today. In those days a Kandyan's best friend was his dagger, and next came his bow and the short-shafted bronze-tipped arrows which the Portuguese, four centuries ago, called "whispering death." Even before the Portuguese, Kandy had its fair share of trouble, and many a king of Uda Rata rode against the Tamil invaders from South India. One of these, a proud youth who had disobeyed his father, hid in exile, and trained an army of guerillas in the jungles. When he was ready he rode against his Tamil enemy, singled him out in battle and slew him. He celebrated his victory by commanding a dance. This was, perhaps, the first time Kandyan dancing was performed. The dancers were granted lands in perpetuity and the descendants of the first Kandyan dancers live today in the villages of Nittawella and Amunugama, which have been theirs for over a thousand years.

Tradition is born of pride and time, so every year in August, when the moon is full, Kandy celebrates the victory of her disobedient son with a Perahera. Feudal chiefs and dancers, elephants decked in cloth-of-gold, torch-bearers and drummers, walk in procession round the town in honor of a king whose courage sustained his people, long after his bones were dust.

To dance at the Raja Maha Perahera, as it is called, is a great honor and every little child of Nittawella and Amunugama stamps his feet for the first time while standing at the bar, hoping that one day the poetry of his performance will cast a spell over an admiring audience. But many a misty dream fades with the passage of years, and meanwhile there is the dancing-master who demands attention while he chants the rhythm.

Talent is molded into art by practice and discipline, and though all the children of the villages can dance, few reach the pinnacle of perfection which brings the privilege of dancing at the Perahera. It is then that the performance is charged with the electricity of effortless grace and utmost elation. They dance by Royal Command.

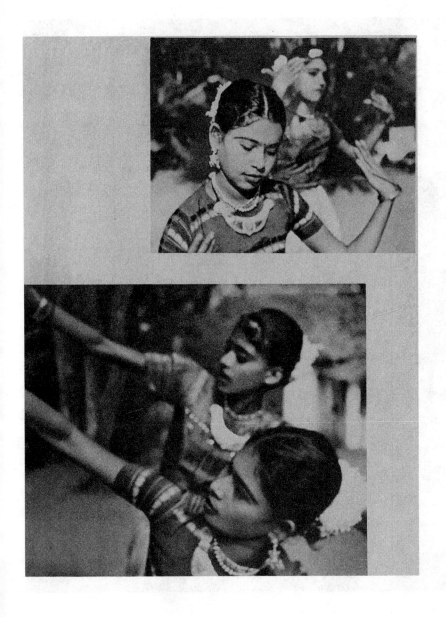

ᛒhe ᛒiᚠᛒ oᚠ ᚪ ᚷoᛑ

History is a measure of the memory of mankind. Princes and paupers, loving or malevolent, tread the corridors of man's time on earth. They fashioned the fate of nations, withstood the onslaughts of nature, and perhaps unconsciously carved for themselves the indelible image of remembrance. They fought for their place in the pages of history, with the bold fervor of belief, or the dry mockery of deceit, and if their tombs are unknown, their presence is felt to this day.

So it was in Lanka, when a prince named Mahinda met a king named Tissa in a forest as old as the earth, and persuaded the king to embrace a new faith. The faith was the doctrine of the Lord Buddha, and upon his conversion Tissa commanded that a shrine be built on the very spot of their meeting. From that day on, the story of Lanka tells of kings and architects who fashioned shrines and temples to the glory of the gentle faith.

But the travelers' tales of cities and palaces, of gold and rubies and sapphires attracted the attention of many a lustful invader. Great wars were fought and great men emerged to fight them. In those days the qualities of kings were judged by their ability in the arts of war, and their wisdom in the ways of peace. Gemunu the Disobedient was possessed of both, and it was he who freed the land of a foreign king, and turned his armies to the task of consolidating peace. In the custom of kings, he built a shrine on the plains where he won freedom for his people, and dedicated it to his faith. It stands to this day, rising above a city that was holy before Gemunu himself was born.

The story of the land continues for over twenty centuries, telling of war and peace, of heroism and cowardice. A host of kings added to it with the color of courage and statesmanship. Gaja Bahu squeezed water from a stone, to convince a Cholean prince that he had better release captured Sinhalese soldiers. Kasyapa coveted his father's wealth, and failing to find it, walled him up alive, and Prakrama the Great built an inland sea which still waters the rice-fields of his people.

But the pride of princes begets their damnation. Civil war and invasion sapped the strength of the people. The splendid cities were sacked and the bunds of the great "wewas" were breached. The destruction that war left unfinished, disease completed.

Quietly the jungle crept over the work of kings, and the bathing pools of queens became the wallow of the wild buffalo.

As the years passed, other visitors came to the land. Some stayed awhile, but all left something of value for the people. Today, as in the time of Tissa, the people offer flowers at the shrines of the gentle faith. They make yearly pilgrimages to the holy cities and practice the customs and traditions born of their ancient heritage. The ruins still stand on the edge of the jungle, their statues sitting in silent conversation. Gone is the splendor of the past. Now there is silence and peace.

ᵹhe Oᴌᴅesᵹ Ciᵹy

Where the foothills rise and swell, the face of the land changes from the lazy lowland plain and crinkles into craggy mountains, split and tortured by countless streams. This is a holy place, where jagged peaks, veiled in mist, are clothed with a forest of incalculable age. There is mystery in these trees, and in their tunnels of deep gloom, hung with wet green moss and dank with the scent of rotting leaves. The underbrush, thick and thorny, grows with ferocity, turning and twisting in every direction to reach the few dim bars of diluted sunlight that penetrate to the forest floor. These matted shrubs fight for life where the competition for bare existence depends upon the ability to shove and bully, thrust and reach. The great trees rise above the tangled mass and take no part in their terrified existence. They climb straight as a ship's mast to the sky and, when in full reach of the sun, their trunks branch into the arms that bear the leaves which keep the gigantic bodies alive. This is the roof of the forest where kites build their nests, and comfortable quarters are rented in snug corners of branch and shade to families of squirrels and whole tribes of nomad monkeys. Of all the forest this is the hardest level to reach, for it is far from the vicious struggle below, and is shrouded in an atmosphere of aristocratic ease and security. These are the penthouses that look down and along the teeming slums of undergrowth.

Lianas, thick as a man's thigh, trail from tree to tree and to the ground, forming arches that would give dignity to a cathedral. They make gloomy corridors, elevated throughways for the flocks of parrakeets and hornbills who dart in search of berries and nesting places. Orioles arc their flight, with wings flashing like sunlight off a mirror, and entire squadrons of red and yellow butterflies flit delicately about their business, pausing only to drink from the flowers. Below begins the writhing tangle of underbrush, thick with thorns and heavy metallic leaves, the home of those who do not care for the light and clean air above them. Snakes and centipedes build underworld burrows beneath rocks covered with mossy slime. Frogs stare with bulging eyes at the dragonflies and spiders weave a delicate web to ensnare the hordes of buzzing insects.

Elephants build roads here, clearing the gloomy tenements of twigs and tendrils, as a bulldozer clears away rubble. Buffalo wallow to the snout in the mud-pools, like down-and-out colonels buried in the armchair memories of long-ago battles. Spotted deer, delicate and dainty, tread warily, like little girls afraid of soiling their crisp party dresses, and jungle fowl and peacocks call like slatternly women berating a new neighbor.

When the new day sends its first warm streak of light to touch the treetops, flocks of painted stork fly in to feed on the mud flats. They march in single file, preoccupied as advertising executives weighing the possibilities of a new account. Egrets, still foggy with sleep stand and stare at the water's edge, much as a man stares at his tousled head and whiskered chin in his bathroom mirror, before making up his mind to shave. As the day progresses the forest prepares for work. Elephants trudge down to the water-holes to drink and bathe, while herds of wild swine plough up acres of mud flats in search of food. Flocks of pelicans and darters maneuver through harbors of lily pads, fishing and quarreling. Leopards prepare to hunt, and deer and sambhur flinch as they sense the unseen form working towards the flanks of the herd.

When the day is spent and night comes, those who have survived the traps and pit-falls seek their homes, and fireflies come out to flash like glowing neon signs.

Forests such as this are the oldest cities in the world, and it was in these secret places that history began.

A WAY OF BEING

Moonrise in the jungle is a thing of quiet splendor. After sunset the sky turns deep blue and clouds fade from livid red to a somber purple, and then, slowly, over the rim of the trees the moon appears. At first it hangs over the horizon glowing and golden and then, when it has climbed the vault of the sky it touches the clouds with silver, and casts quaint shadows on familiar things.

There is a place where the moonlight touches a humpbacked pile of granite that rises sheer on all sides above the lowland forests. At nightfall strange sounds are heard in the vicinity of this rock and the people of the little village who live not far away know that their wood god is abroad. To them he is very real and omnipotent. He is a god without form or name or shrine, yet the stretch of jungle where the village and the "wewa" and the pile of granite lie, is his. It is he who climbs the unscaleable rock to beat a drum at night, and the throbbing rhythm of it can be heard above the sawing of the cicadas and the coughing growl of the leopards who lie in wait. He is a formless ghost, a *thing*, who holds sway of life and death over those who enter his domain.

Not far from this humpbacked pile of granite, five hills clothed in twisted, thorn-spiked trees that draw their nourishment from the parched red earth, thrust five jagged peaks into the sky. This is a forbidding place of tumbled rocks that shelter many bear, and deep ravines where cobras and vipers make their homes. Gigantic anthills hard as steel give shelter, not only to the termites, but also to the monstrous monitor-lizards that look like some forgotten primeval demon, but are completely harmless. Near here is the River of Jewels—the Menik Ganga—shaded by towering kumbuk trees, whose roots writhe as though in agony. It is here that the most powerful God of all projects the power of his presence along every footpath and every nook of sun and shade. This is the home of the Kataragama God. He is a God of many forms, yet without form, of many names yet without a name. He was born of fire at a time when gods walked among men and waged wars of thunder and lightning against oppressive giants. One day he made a journey on a granite raft that floated on a milky ocean and visited Lanka. The smell of the drying fish on the beach so offended his nostrils that he hurled his spear into the sky and where it fell the spot was sacred. Thus it was that the shrine in the jungle came into being, for the God, when he went to retrieve his spear, fell in love with a beautiful girl, the foster child of a veddha chief, and married her.

His power has grown with the passage of years, and he has witnessed the events that shaped much of the island's history. The Lord Buddha is said to have visited the place of his shrine, and kings have begged his blessing on the eve of battle.

Today his influence is felt over Asia and pilgrims from places far off journey to his shrine to do penance and ask his favor. He demands a faith almost superhuman and the acts of penance performed by his followers indicate the limits to which they are possessed of him. Only through suffering can a soul achieve perfection; the greater the pain, the nearer the goal. To believe, to renounce the world, to reach for the treasure of the mind, no longer influenced by the sensations of the body in which it is imprisoned, to experience the ecstasy of oneness with Creation, this is the goal of the true believer. His is not a way of life—it is a way of being.

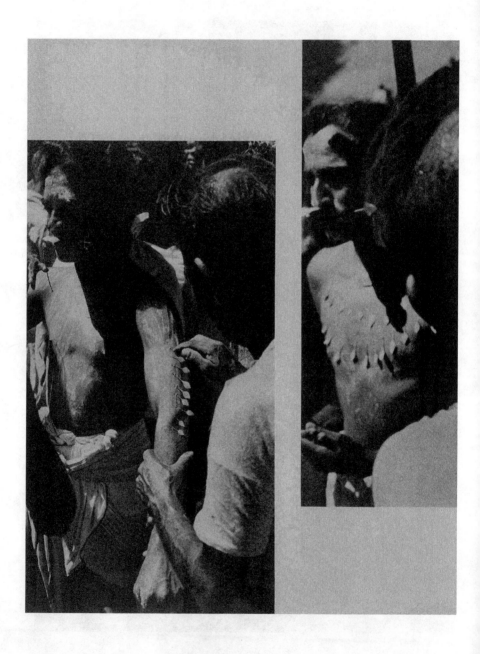

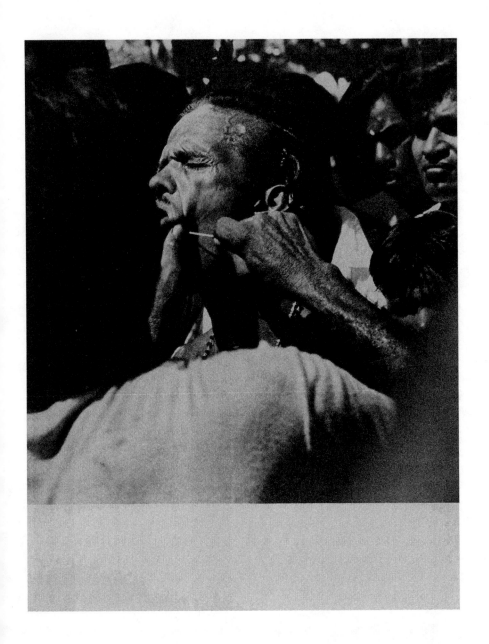

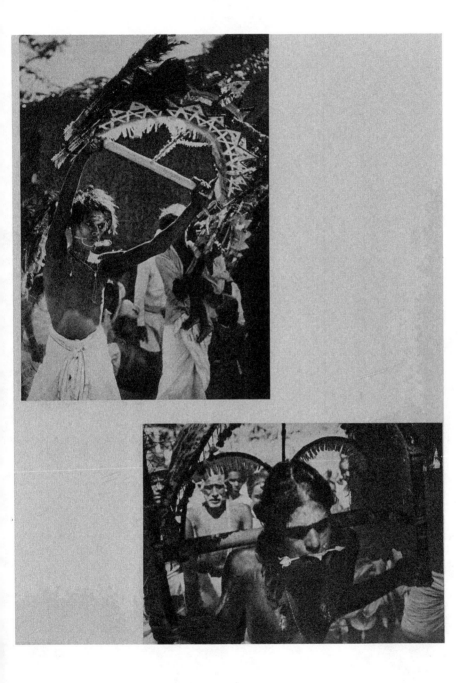

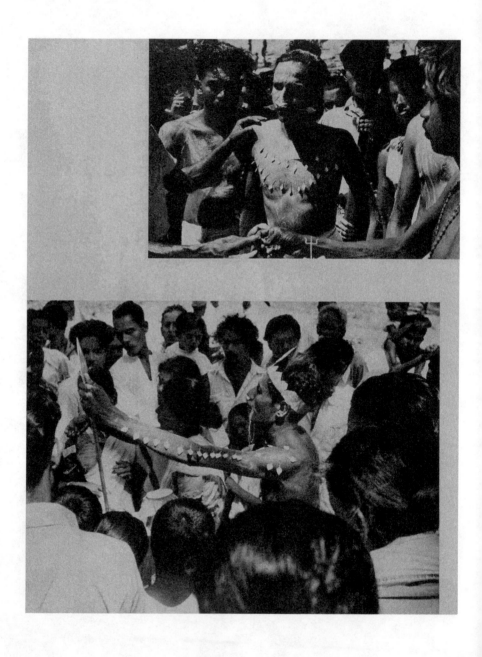

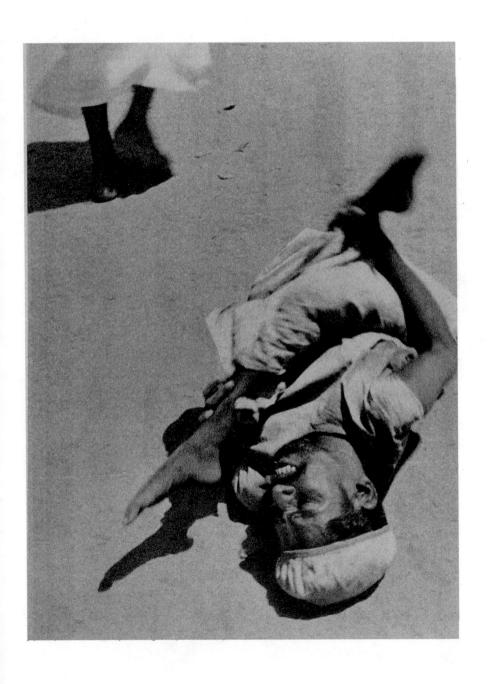

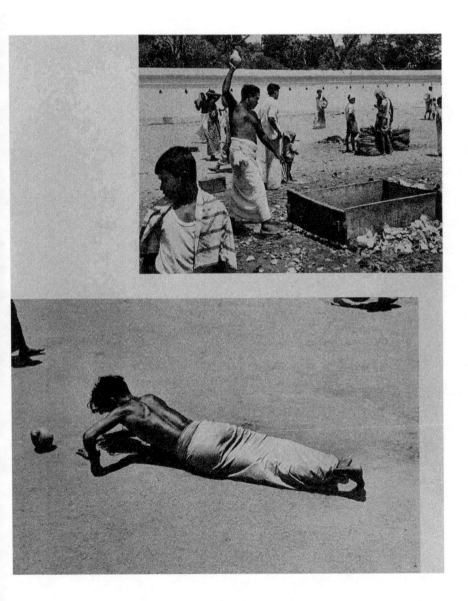

The Forces of Destruction

All things change, and all life must end. Mortal forms, once swollen with life, shrink and die and crumble, to pay back to the earth that bore them the debts incurred in life.

In this city of the forest the laws are made by Nature, who controls the forces which put them into operation. Too often, the mind of man is unable to understand the justice of which he bears witness. The path of life is mapped and measured from birth to death. To those who dwell in the forest this is the reason for the drought that dries up waterholes into slimy pools thick with scum and polluted with carrion; for the floods that wash away entire villages, and change the course of old rivers, and for death, which of all things is inevitable.

Even in disease and loneliness the laws of Nature bring justice and mercy, for there are some for whom the burden of life is too great to bear. So the wheel turns full circle, and those who in life walked in fear and hatred, meet in death, and with the dust of their bodies give nourishment to the earth from which all life springs. Thus it was written, thus shall it ever be.

The Forces of Life

To every fawn and fledgling, and every fruit and flower, the gift of life brings the adventure of growth and the will to survive. Young animals grow from helpless trembling things to adventurous adolescents and finally into responsible adults who have families of their own, and school their young in the arts of survival. Tender shoots spring from tiny seeds and grow into the tall trees whose purpose is to provide shelter and bring rain.

During their growth the architecture of nature manifests itself in form and structure which gives the strength required for life and being. Banyan trees buttress their great branches with aerial roots and slender grasses divide their pliant bodies in perfect symmetry to reach water and sunlight. Growth is a desperate thing and is accomplished with a feverish intensity and an iron will. Seeds so small that their size belies their strength give birth to saplings whose tender trunks split great rocks apart, to bear their branches to the light. Life is good and must be lived with enjoyment and freedom, for who can say when the span will end, and the gift of wealth be taken away?

Meanwhile great clouds reflect in brimming rice-fields and the earth is rich.

AN ABUNDANT OCEAN

There is a time of year, when days dawn bright and crisp, and the sky is without cloud from noon till nightfall. This is the time when the smell of the sea is strong, for the wind blows inland, loaded with salt and the smell of sails and fresh-caught fish. The sea is green and lazy except along the shoreline where occasional waves swell and curve and crash against the orange sand, as if to indicate that it is storing its energy for some important task. Little knots of women and children stand along the beach, their eyes focussed on the far horizon. There is an air of expectancy in their attitude. Suddenly someone shouts and points, and on the horizon a little speck appears, which soon resolves into a square sail swollen with wind, and borne shorewards by the life of the sea. The fishermen are coming home.

One by one the fleet comes in, riding over the reef into the surf where the boats run aground and lines of men strain at the ropes to pull them ashore. There is great excitement everywhere. Children rush into the water to greet their fathers. Nets heavy with fish are emptied onto the sand and shrieking gulls hover and swoop to steal what they can. The women sort and gut the fish. Some of it is sold on the spot, the rest prepared for salting, or carried away to market in large wicker baskets. The menfolk, spent and weary, coil nets and ropes, then make for their huts and a long draught of palm-toddy. Soon the beach is deserted save for the boats which stand on the sand, their sails drying in the wind, and the gulls swooping for morsels of offal.

The life of the fishermen is not an easy one. Their incredible little craft, made of jak-wood and held together by coir rope and copper nails sail far out to sea in search of the shoals of seer and parauw. Once out, they are at the mercy of sun and wind. The men who sail them pit skill and strength against the elements, to wrest from the ocean the harvest by which they live.

It is in the nature of islands to breed this kind of man, for however rich and fertile the land may be, there are those who prefer the distant view of waves to the cramped confines of fields. So these men, who cannot guide a plough and who do not know the language of the water-buffalo and the elephant, make their homes on the shores of crescent bays and haunted lagoons. Here they build their boats and mend their nets, and wait for the wind to swell their sails.

I know a village of half-a-dozen huts built on a pencil of land where a lagoon, fringed with mangrove and scrub-jungle, meets the sea. During the long hot months of drought a bar of sand seals the mouth of the lagoon, and the sun exposes acres of mud-flats, split into great scabrous cracks, into which scorpions crawl for shelter. Painted stork and pelicans fish industriously in the shallows, while far out across the water mother elephants squirt their babies clean. Fishing eagles build their nests in twisted trees, in whose gnarled bodies there runs more salt than sap, and at dawn, their calls carry to the village.

The men set out to sea very early, and the women are busy salting the catch of the previous day. Children armed with harpoons pole their little outriggers through the mangroves, looking for sting-rays, or stand and fling their throw-nets which flash and swirl and drop with a silver splash. All through the day they labor, pausing only to collect the fish from their nets. As the sun climbs higher the water sparkles with a million diamonds, and the heat blackens their skin. Afternoon lengthens into evening, and the sky turns pink and purple and emerald. The egrets and pelicans call to each other before settling in the trees, and whistling teal fly in formation high in the evening sky. The children return to the village and the women prepare the evening meal, while the men sit on the sand in a half-circle in front of a little fire.

This is story-telling time, and one old tale tells of a certain queen who came from South India to buy bushels of pearls from a pearl-fishery not far from the village, a long, long time ago. The pearls had to be of perfect quality, color, and shape, and the only man who had such gems was a brave and handsome young diver, with whom she fell deeply in love. But the queen's jealous husband, who was as ugly as a toad, heard of her love for the pearl-diver, so he called his warriors and sailed to the village and destroyed it. A great battle was fought in which the handsome young diver was slain, and that is why, the fishermen say, the sand of the beach is as red as blood, in the rays of the setting sun, for the diver gave his life for his love and his land.

Date Due		
JY 10 '67		
SE 30 '70		
OC 15 '70		
OC 30 '70		
NO 13 '70		
JE 28 '71		
	PRINTED IN U. S. A.	

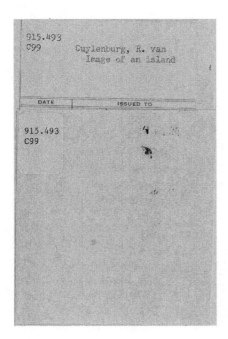